T0200787

In Darwin's Room

ALSO BY DEBORA GREGER

Movable Islands (1980)

And (1985)

The 1002nd Night (1990)

Off-Season at the Edge of the World (1994)

Desert Fathers, Uranium Daughters (1996)

God (2001)

Western Art (2004)

Men, Women, and Ghosts (2008)

By Herself (2012)

In Darwin's Room

Debora Greger

PENGUIN POETS

PENGUIN BOOKS

An imprint of Penguin Random House LLC
375 Hudson Street
New York, New York 10014
penguin.com

Copyright © 2017 by Debora Greger
Penguin supports copyright. Copyright fuels creativity, encourages diverse voices, pro-
motes free speech, and creates a vibrant culture. Thank you for buying an authorized
edition of this book and for complying with copyright laws by not reproducing, scan-
ning, or distributing any part of it in any form without permission. You are supporting
writers and allowing Penguin to continue to publish books for every reader.

LIBRARY OF CONGRESS CATALOGING-IN-PUBLICATION DATA
Names: Greger, Debora, 1949- author.
Title: In Darwin's room / Debora Greger.
Description: New York, New York : Penguin Books, 2017. | Series: Penguin poets
Identifiers: LCCN 2016055453 (print) | LCCN 2016055536 (ebook) | ISBN
9780143131311 (paperback) | ISBN 9781524705053 (e-book)
Subjects: | BISAC: POETRY / American / General.
Classification: LCC PS3557.R42 A6 2017 (print) | LCC PS3557.R42 (ebook) | DDC 811/.54—dc23
LC record available at https://lccn.loc.gov/2016055453

Printed in the United States of America
1   3   5   7   9   10   8   6   4   2

Set in Electra LT Std
Designed by Ginger Legato

in memory of my father and mother

Greg Greger (1923–2015)
Margaret Greger (1923–2009)

CONTENTS

I

II

III

IV

No *poet ever felt more delight at seeing his first poem pub-
lished than I did at seeing in Stephens'* Illustrations of British
Insects *the magic words, "captured by C. Darwin, Esq."*

—AUTOBIOGRAPHY OF CHARLES DARWIN, 1887

*Never did I think so highly of our present Government, as
when I heard they had selected Charles Darwin for Gt. naturalist
& that he was to be trans-ported (with pleasure of course)
for 3 years— Woe unto ye Beetles of South America, woe unto
all tropical butterflies.*

—FREDERICK WATKINS, SEPTEMBER 18, 1831

What we gain by science is, after all, sadness.

—THOMAS HARDY

I

Then I went back into the house and wrote, It is midnight.
The rain is beating on the windows. It was not midnight. It
was not raining.

—SAMUEL BECKETT

In the Museum of Recent Time

this morning hasn't been unpacked.
But here lie the last hundred thousand years:
tray upon tray of fossils dug and scrubbed
until—like day-old bakery goods—
petrified snails, stony heart-shaped shells
harden to history. A handful of sand
traveled from a place spelled out
with finest nib in letters too small to read,
yellowed paper given a special fold
so not a grain was lost between then

and the afternoon I saw a woman crouch
in a museum, unlock a drawer,
and dust her way through a geological age
endured until closing time—

as if yesterday a young man sat,
cramped in his cabin, seasick,
doggedly logging another rock.
But first he gave it a lick, as he'd been taught.
C. Darwin, Esq., I've seen your sample
of South America, so nondescript it's mysterious—

like the pebbles I picked up as a kid
from the river that drifted through childhood
as if it had all day. They dried into dullness,
the way all the adults I knew did,
even the agate, even the quartz.

The Last Dodo of Iowa

In the Midwest of memory,
no fence sags, no sign rusts.
A tin ear of corn with wings still flies
over a field bleak as blackboard.

There's that tapping:
a student poet x-ing out something
and then pounding it back again.
In the fat Russian novel that was Iowa,

pages went blank, the wind
binding one snowy signature to another.
My hand to your cheek—which was colder?
You stood at the door of winter,

Milky Way spilling ancient history.
What did you want?
When I should have been writing,
I stood in the ratty museum

of natural history under long bones
of a right whale hung from the ceiling.
How had it washed up in a place so wrong?
Whalebone floated over a songbird

whose wing had been broken,
then folded as flat as an envelope.
A small cloud of cotton oozed from the eye.
A tag tied to the twig of a leg

gave the place of capture: *Yakima.*
Bird, I have been to that far corner
of the West since you were taken.
Sawmills stand on their last board feet,

first growth gone, second, too;
but orchards and packing-houses are still there—
I turned, and looked a dodo in the glass eye.

On First Looking into Darwin's Microscope

Behind glass, it squatted,
knobby wallaby of brass,
pouch gaping where a specimen belonged.
A book lay open to the creatures
he called "my beloved cirripedia."

Oh, unlovely barnacles,
have I loved anything as much?
On the Pacific of a blank page,
he drew a tidy archipelago of extinct volcanoes,
pleating and plumping stiff Victorian skirts

into escarpments, the latest fashions for 1853.
Next door, moons scurried, planets crawled,
gears of an orrery grinding away
at the long-abandoned Julian calendar.
Down its gnomon, a pocket sundial,

case cracked open like a peach,
peered into artificial light:
in a schoolhouse turned mausoleum,
my tread made a compass needle quaver.
One pan of a scale slumped, needing a hand

to lift the dust gathered mote by mote.
There it waited to be asked to measure
eternity in apothecary's scruples,
a twenty-fourth of an ounce at a time.

Expression of Emotion in Man and Insects

Under glass, a forest of pins
held down an army of insects:
dung-beetle tanks, armored cars, caissons and carts

towing white flags that bore fancy names
they'd been given by the conqueror,
and dates of capture. The smallest,

collected when Darwin was a young man
neglecting divinity study,
lay where they'd been glued to their tags,

waiting for stretcher-bearers. On the other side
of the island, at the end of an aisle of skeletons,
I found finches a long way from home—

long dead, sooty feathers sewn shut
over wads of wool, feet tied with thread
into a faded bouquet of twigs and dance cards.

When I'd opened the door of the museum
devoted to every kind but my own,
the scent of salvation had nearly defeated me:

moth flakes fighting to kill the living
to keep them from feasting on the dead.

In Darwin's Room

at his old college, they chipped away
the twenty-first century. And the twentieth:
gone, the sixties upholstery,
and the thirties from the window seat.
How old the horse whose hair had stuffed it?

The strict grass of the Great Court lay
in the sixteenth century. But up the staircase,
a room awaited a young man who'd be ravenous
after an afternoon of prying up bark
in search of beetles—though, to the ugly rug,

now rewoven, no clay, as if from his boots,
had been added. In the dregs of daylight,
one November afternoon, 1829,
he wrote out his father's objections
to a son taking voyage on a ship named for a dog:

Disreputable to my character as a Clergyman hereafter.
A wild scheme.
That they must have offered to many others before me
the place of Naturalist. And from its not being accepted
there must be some serious objection to the vessel or expedition.

That I should never settle down to a steady life hereafter.
That my accommodations would be most uncomfortable.
That you should consider it as again changing my profession.
That it would be a useless undertaking.

To a Mockingbird by the Rappahannock

I.

There's a tobacconist and confectioner.
A clothier for the lady of leisure
who lunches at the inn, then plays a round of golf

on the hill where Lee's gray men spent winter,
1862, her cleats in the footsteps of ghosts.
We're a block from a river

the Battle of Fredericksburg left red,
on a street where North fought South
through colonial houses, room to room.

In beribboned front parlors,
bookseller, baker—each has a barrel
of bullets by the door, the price for a handful

of spent lead nubbins marked down again.

II.

Mockingbird, you're the same unearthed ash,
a handful of lead and dirt.
Yet of cell phone and car alarm you sing.

Your bloodless night lies where it fell in the river
until, under the sting of stars,
some graybeard raises a lantern.

Someone follows the dog of darkness
from one stench to the ghost of another,
still looking for his brother.

The dead have had enough.
Where's the real poet, they demand,
the one who brought tea and tobacco,

brandy, peaches, oysters, and socks
to the makeshift hospital on the hill?
Take these leaves America, a mockingbird sings.

On First Looking into Chapman's *Flora*

A. W. Chapman,
Flora of the Southern United States, 1860

Little have I traveled in the realm of dirt.
So the cypress has knees with which to breathe?
Sweet gum, what good your Latin name,
I say, who barely remember your common one.

Vine taking back the front flower bed,
in the time it took me to open his book,
you sent a tendril over the porch rail,
over my shoulder, to turn the page.

Foxed, dog-eared, torn and taped,
re-bound in red buckram—
Dr. Chapman, Northern transplant,
would have loved this much-loved copy.

Someone who slogged to page 184
despaired of identifying a leaf
and pressed it there instead.
Only a tannic stain remains.

I felt like some watcher of the dirt
who missed the faint impress
of hobnail boot. Do cushions still
lie low in a box pew of the oldest church

in Apalachicola? The doctor wanted comfort,
nights he hid from men in gray

searching the dark for supplies. A slave watched
his arsenic and chloroform while he slept,

a Northerner wanted by a South
whose wounds he didn't care to bind.

Keats to a Young Poet of the Seventies

I think of the Elgin Marbles,
how many men it would take
to wrestle the wreck of my heart
on board ship in the Bay of Naples
so by the greasy Thames it might lie.

Consider the ox that tugs at the heart,
great cords of its neck ropy with strain:
first, it learned to listen to the lash,
till power to answer back was all it lacked.
The horse brought from the field forgot its mother,

going up and down instead for a master.
It stands in the stable, fearing the lash.
When you despair, blank paper pleases,
if not more than a clean shirt.
Must you rush to see foreign flowers?

I did, and cared not a straw for them.
Oh, to see again the muddied blooms
of English spring! Would that I were
a sort of ethereal pig turned out to feed
upon them—I the wingèd thing that lived

but three summer days.

From *The Britanniad*

I. *Thrush's Song*

King of the alley that runs behind England,
I sing the rat who feeds on the garbage of heaven.
From the top of a tree no one planted,
I smooth the air, lord of all I survey.

I do not sing your garden snail or his lies.
I pound his shell on a rock and feast—
but not yet. The epic journey of a day
goes nowhere, at great length, as Homer proved.

How can you lie abed? Sing the vestment of frost
and the soul's finical trail of slime,
pearly under the morning star.
Medlar and sloe sweeten in decay.

II. *House Spider's Odyssey*

What is a sleeve but poor imitation
of the silk funnel I've yet to spin
in some dark corner of your life?
From the eye of a buttonhole

in a shirt abandoned on a chair,
I watch your beloved sleep on the couch,
mouth ajar. I watch TV for hours,
yet no actor needs eight legs to come through a door.

None rappels down a living room wall.
When male finds female in a wee hour,
how can he nuzzle at lips the color of meat?
Long ago this morning, I drank my fill

from a dripping faucet, then scaled the white cliffs
of kitchen sink. Steering by lightbulbs,
I crossed the lunar seas of ceiling—
I, Odysseus, called the cunning, the wanderer.

Flora Americana

I. Natives

With mattock and machete, with Spanish
when those failed, a man attacked the hedge.
Before the neighbor's azaleas could bloom
into ball gowns or bishops' robes—before
I could say *sunset hung on a bush to dry*—

men gouged them out. In bare dirt,
seeds long dormant staked their claim
to all a weed demands.
And earth brought forth vegetation.
And there was evening and there was morning,

a third day. And the landscaper?
No matter. From each unwanted seed,
rude reminder of America's lost Eden.
Beggar-ticks, you pencil-mark my clothes
with seed when I approach—

but next door you host a butterfly. Tell me,
were those the underwing eyespots
of an American painted lady I saw?
Weed, may I call you wildflower?

II. *Invaders*

Dandelion, I beg your pardon.
You're an immigrant like the rest of us?
You've made yourself at home,
root so deep, no gardener digs enough

to halt your spread. What palace grounds
did you *not* invade? You bow
in the court of the wind,
only its empire vaster than yours.

Next to you, the sun grows dull.
Seed-cloud pressed in Gerard's *Herball,*
your fluff crossed the Atlantic in the foolhardy trunk
of a Pilgrim—tell me, commoner,

pissabed, how you stowed away
in livestock fodder, on ballast cobble.

III. *Recipe*

Off with their heads! How much per flower
did Mother pay us to pick the yard clean?
She sweetened, soured, steeped, and strained.
In a dark corner of the laundry room,
a crock huddled under a cloth. Life stank of death.

Water turned to wine—at least to beer.
If the recipe came from Grandmother—
as my sister claims—who passed it to *her*?
What ancestor left the old country
with the scraps she owned

of the rotted nineteenth century?
For, to perfect a dandelion wine,
the English would lay it down for half a year.
But the Irish wait six months for a drink?
They drained dandelion beer after a week—

long enough for water to turn to alcohol.
Left to us: a quilt pieced from necktie slivers,
nothing too narrow to reuse,
silk in shatters. A plump Victorian Bible,
a page crowded with births and deaths

fading to make room for more.
Dandelion, we inherited you.

II

I remember. Don't remember.
Yes! A suit of clothes went past,
uninhabited and hollow,
slaked lime, in among the trees.
I followed . . . Two voices said
there was no one there to follow.

—RAFAEL ALBERTI

Elegy on the Far Bank

in memoriam Greg Greger (1923–2015)

I. *Hard to Say*

His taxes done, a garden planned,
my father didn't want even a night
in the hospital—then he lay his head back
and drifted away from the doctor.

For the first time in days he slept,
better than he had for years.
The coin in his mouth he surrendered
to the ferryman, and crossed a river

he'd never fished. What were we, his children,
but overgrowth crowding the bank he'd left?
Sandbar willow or Russian olive—
hard to say without his glasses.

My breath snagged on a fishhook.
From the gasping lip of something I caught
sixty years ago, he eased a barb.
The rock he forbade me to throw in the water

turned out to have a higher calling: deftly,
he clubbed a fish big enough to eat.
Too small to keep? He loosed it in shallows—
just so, he taught me the dead man's float.

Breath held a word as long as it could.

II. West of Chekhov

A month since Father died. Back in our old house,
sisters, where were we? Desert of childhood,
    great preserver,

for you we opened another closet.
Father the farm boy—what didn't he save?
    There his army jacket

with ribbons we never learned to read.
He left a wooden box of negatives
    in the coal-store.

Studio portraits of ghosts reeked of hypo,
emulsions wrinkled with age, glassine sleeves
    gone yellow.

From the basement a brother emerged
with a hammer, the peen soldered with brass
    to prolong its life.

Open the front door and draw breath!
Cottonwood seed clouds his lawn, his car—
    they to be packed as well.

III. *In the Horse Heavens*

We climbed the Horse Heaven Hills,
   my dead father and I.
Taller than he'd been for decades, bronzed,
   he was sure-footed again,
though you heard the uneven gait
   of someone who'd been thrown
by a horse eight decades before. Left breathless

   by his weakened heart?
No, brushing back waves of hair he'd yet to lose,
   he traced a dark ribbon
of river to a small patch of lights. Farsighted again,
   he said—but a wind
came up and tore his words from me.

IV. *My Parents Return from the Dead*

as from a trip,
needing no luggage—

Father having gone
to the underworld to get Mother.
They look young:

He has hair, she her mind.
Older than they are,
we crowd around the table,

sitting where we always did.
"What's for supper?" the youngest asks
at the open fridge.

He stands, expensive shoes bathed
in milk-blue light
spilled on the scarred linoleum.

Arctic in their purity,
the empty shelves. In the cupboard,
not a dish of dust.

V. *Rockshelter*

Why stop at the end
of nowhere? Down a road unpaved,
through a ranch of scrub, Dad drove us
    to see a cave barely there,

    it was so shallow.
Down a hole crouched a man.
A pie pan offered splintered, filthy finds:
    elk bone,

    bone tools.
Human remains, broken and burned:
oh, ice age, we bring nothing
    into this world.

    My father's ninety years—
down a deep hole, with a dirty toothbrush,
a man will take pains to sweep them away.
    Why stop here ever again?

    The levee built
to protect the site from water swelling
behind a new dam will seep,
    wound unstanched.

Windy Ode

Wind, you haven't changed.
Remember that town you did your best to level?

Trapped in classroom doldrums,
I tried to fashion a W that would set sail

across the page of the penmanship book.
Beyond the dusty horizon, Sister Columba said,

lay the new world of fourth grade,
everything curled in cursive.

Had you carved your mark there?
You staggered down the street

with a tumbleweed on each arm
as if a million prickles made them easier

to slam into a chain-link fence.
Wind, let us be restless together.

Elegy for an English Teacher

How her pin curls would quiver,
punctuation too eloquent for words.

Tonight lightning diagrams a sentence
cantilevered in complexity:

a single stroke divides the dark
into subject and predicate.

On the darker *verso*, it continues.
Remember how she fed us that word?

On the eel of a mouthful that was *soliloquy*,
we choked. In a blizzard of chalk dust,

she filled the blackboard with fourteen lines
to be transcribed. Which play was it from?

We were medieval scribes, laboring the days
before a Xerox machine came to town.

Her virtuous hand—no, her red-nailed,
vulturous claw—rattled the chalk.

Tonight the sky is a blackboard,
badly erased. Mrs. D would not be pleased.

The War After the War

I.

Where were the next-door neighbors?
In pajamas, I sat at my father's feet
before their squat, myopic television,
the first on our street.

On a screen the size of a dinner plate,
toy airplanes droned over quilted fields.
Bouquets of jellyfish fell: parachutes abloom,
toy soldiers drifting together, drifting apart—

the way families do, but I didn't know that yet.
I was six or seven, this an aquarium:
steely fish fell from the belly of a plane,
then burst into flame when they hit.

A dollhouse surrendered a wall, as such houses do.
Furniture clung to wallpaper for dear life.
Down in the crumple of what had been a street,
women tore brick from brick, filling a baby carriage.

II.

A few years back from that war,
what was my young father looking for?
Once he'd been a farm boy from Nebraska.
Once he'd seen Dachau.

Back home, my brother and sister fought
the Battle of Bedtime, bath by bath.
In the living room, a two-tone cowboy lay
where he fell, too bowlegged to stand.

Where was his horse? The Indian
who'd come apart at the waist—
where were his legs? A fireman,
licorice-red from helmet to boot,

white rope around his arm like a mint Life Saver,
tried to help. A few inches of ladder
crawled under a cushion, looking for crumbs.
Between sagging couch and slumped rocker,

past a pickle-green soldier,
a plastic foxhole dug into the rug
and waited to trip my mother.

III.

Am I the oldest here? The cave
of a cinema smelled of mouse and mold.
Cell phone screens constellated the dark
with their empty light-years.

And then we were in Algiers, we were in Marseille.
On foot, we fell in behind a ragged file
of North African infantry. Farther north
than they'd ever been, we trudged

into the arms of the enemy: winter, 1944.
Why did the French want to live in France,
the youngest wondered while they hid,
awaiting capture by the cold.

They relieved a dead German of greatcoat and boots.
Village by muddy village, they stole,
shadow to shadow, trying to last
until the Americans arrived—

as if, just out of range of the lens,
open trucks of my father's unit
would rumble over the rutted horizon.
Good with a rifle, farsighted farm boy

made company clerk because he'd learned to type
in high school—how young he'd look,

not half my age, and no one to tell him
he'd survive those months in Europe,

be spared the Pacific by Hiroshima.
Fifty years later, from the drawer
where he kept the TV remote,
he'd take a small gray notebook

and show his eldest daughter
how, in pencil, in tiny hurried script,
he kept the names of those who died around him.

Surplus Poem

Solitudinem fecerunt, pacem appelunt.

—TACITUS

In the corner of Basin Surplus,
    a snake of rope
coiled in wait: thick as the arm
    of the eight-year-old
I would turn the following week,
    it gathered dust—
no, that took effort. In the heat,
    it knew a quarter
burned a hole in my pocket:
    the week's allowance.
What did I have to tie up, anyhow,
    but the baby
Mother had brought home?
    Wasn't one brother enough?

Bayonets unstuck from their guns,
    canteens filled with air
some other desert had wrung dry—
    oh, where was my father
after the war? As if from a trench,
    he peered over a bank
of mutant trigger-finger mittens.
    Only he could see
an entrenching tool digging for clams—
    if we drove to the coast.

Downwind from the reactor
   baking a fresh batch
of weapons-grade plutonium,
   we made a desert
out of family and called it peace.

My First Museum

boasted one room. Walls bristled with arrowheads:
a dentist had spread his collection on cotton,
flints turned to flower petals.

Across rectangular cloud, birdpoints so small
they might have been toys flew in a V,
a flock of geese heading home forever.

Below them, under glass, a skeleton lay,
a dusty point embedded in the spine.
Had the dentist dug up a burial mound?

The bones were dirtier than I expected.
Around a breath no longer held,
grubby ribs still cupped themselves,

the way my girlish fingers tried to trap water.
Curled in the dust like a cur in the dark cave
of eye socket, nothing hid.

May Altar Constructed from Memory

God lay down in the one cool spot
    of the hall.
Down He lay, one eye closed,
    one keeping watch,
for we'd been given leave to retire
    the wool uniform.
In the desert of grade school,
    in the heat,
we could dress like Protestants
    for a month—
but covered. Upholstered.
    On Mother's Day,
the priest poured fire and brimstone
    on spaghetti straps.

Sister Innocentia turned a desk
    into an altar
for a plaster Virgin who stomped a snake.
    She accepted
our homegrown flowers, even bedraggled.
    The dry air
of learning grew sinful with scent.
    A pencil sharpened
filled the room with cedars felled in the fight
    with square roots.
Abandoned in the cloakroom,
    a banana blackened

like the dubious finger of a saint.
    I was rusting—
I could smell it in my sweaty palm.

    In pickle jars,
carnal flowers leaned from each other,
    into the martyr's sin.
Silk and velvet, tongue and beard,
    they lusted.
They were bent on dying.

My Brief Reign

I, the eldest, exalted myself
over boredom and the others—
over all but the baby, our new brother.
Thirteen, I crowned myself
with a wreath that turned out too loose.

Cottonwoods whispered rumors
of kingdoms somewhere—of countries
unseen except in classrooms
where maps pulled down like blinds
to hide the world from us.

How could my empire be overrun
by September massing on the horizon?
I commanded a lawn chair be set in the shade.
I called for a goblet of purple Kool-Aid,
the hue reserved for royalty.

From the front porch, I ruled over all
but the new baby in the kingdom of Indoors,
whose tiny fist crushed something I failed to grasp.
A quarter we charged neighbors
to see us play *The Emperor's New Clothes*

before we surrendered to school.
Who did I think I was? A girl in red pajamas
or emperor in his invisible suit?
A needle threaded with nothing
whipped ragged edges together.

Prelude and Fugue for Desert Winds

I.

Breezy companion of my fourteenth year,
who had the breathier voice?

Father had found you in a classified.
For twenty-five dollars, what did I expect?

How close we were for a year,
you suffering my wordless exhalations,

me wrapping myself around your hollowness.
You the door the wind cut:

in rushed the needled sigh of pines.
A blue mountain drew near,

meltwater braiding runs and trills
flooding the muddy air of the practice room.

Someone else's breath had worn away your silver.
Kidskin keypads had shriveled,

making notes harder to hit, Teacher explained.
Everything went dry in that desert.

Flute, where are you now?

II.

I praise the way he conducted us,
first into stillness, then to an A

that fluttered, flame trying to catch,
as if he'd forgotten the early hour,

the mystery burning in the cafeteria,
the scent of some furtive failure

I couldn't catch. How had he ended up
in that sad suit, trying to hold the eyes

of children of nuclear engineers?
We played the fugue just once, sight-reading,

handing the theme around the room,
winds to reeds to brass—Johann Sebastian,

how bad were we? Did your kapellmeister bones
turn over in far-off German dirt?

I heard footsteps, someone whistling as he walked
to the edge of a small town and kept going

into wilderness thick with crotchets and quavers.

The Later Martyrs

Night, why have you drawn this empty net
from your dry depths for me?
What do I want

with a cat's-eye marble, once my brother's?
Let its sleeping planet lie
in the weeds

of the empty lot where the past once stood.
A blue petal of broken glass
is all that's left

of a bottle of ink. And that animal, leathery scent—
a brush of my father's hands?
No, his old satchel.

It ate my homework with a dark, satanic yawn.
Into its cavernous maw I fed the bottle,
willing it not to spill.

Down the block, the book bag nipped at my heels.
It swung at stop sign, fence, and tree;
it slapped my leg.

Onto my desk I flopped the dead fish of it.
I traced the initials stamped in gold.
The letters gave up guarding the clasp

and I reached—into broken glass.
On school uniform and catechism
how soulfully my blood spilled!

But, Sister Sebastian said
to a class that longed for the fires of hot lunch,
we were forbidden to wish for martyrdom.

Did she have visions of a crossroads
where pleasure collided with pain?
This is not for her.

This is for a Quaker and for a Buddhist monk.
A few years later, despairing of war
in a tiny country

I'd never heard of, they would turn themselves
into flame instead of into prayer,
one in Washington, one in Saigon.

To Myself, Then

Whoever you were, step outside
so I can see you. From the dark house,
last before thistles take over
the vacant lot of the future,

step into a wind that has roughed up the river.
It scrapes cloud across moon—
oh, to feel that sandy tongue lick my face again!
In the dragged-out desert of your teens,

you barely raise your dirt-brown eyes.
You kick a tumbleweed to the horizon
you've drawn in the dust—then
there's nowhere to go but back to your room.

Paris could be on the far side of the moon,
somewhere past Seattle. Night has nothing
to lean on but the bedroom windowsill,
slack-jawed. What were you playing

in the depths of the house? The secondhand piano—
how much of the world had it traveled,
only to end up spray-painted puce
by Father to hide the scrapes?

Through an ebony underbrush of minor keys
crashed the ghost of a great tusked creature,
scales descending in staggers to the ground.

Double Self-Portrait, Pinned Together

I. *Exterior with Pincushion*

Whoever you were, you stepped out of the house,
out of your life: on the front porch

at twelve, a girl poked the steely eye
of a needle. Even summer had tired of me.

Thread refusing to watch where it was going,
I stabbed at cloth until it was embroidered

with small red planets of finger blood.
I was Sleeping Beauty, torn like silk

between desire to be bandaged,
desire to hide from Mother's call for bed.

I rose, bare foot forgetting a pincushion
sat beside me. Over sunset's glittery gash,

nighthawks pinned a worn sheet of sky.

II. *Interior with Pincushion*

The room kept silent,
furniture ready to flee

the minute a needle glinted,
unsheathed by the acupuncturist.

On the table I lay, meat sinking into itself.
I was allowed to move my eyes:

out the window, steam rose after rain.
Leaves of live oak gleamed like lard.

I thought of a length of firewood I'd seen,
sleek, unlikely log that, when I stopped,

turned into an otter beside the highway,
viscid with death. Carelessly,

a mockingbird threw song's gray rag
over my pierced flesh.

The Family Silence

in memoriam Timothy Greger (1948)

A hill came out of nowhere.
My dead brother said nothing;
he never did. Where was he leading us?

Up. On a night this clear, you could see
the broken bracelet of a small town
at our feet. Beads of headlights unstrung

rolled down a black ribbon of river.
Sixty years of silence had turned his voice
to the whisper of cottonwoods.

*You're right: you don't want to come back
until you're dead,* he said,
who died at birth. *Then everything looks new.*

The family silence trailed at my heels,
doggedly sniffing other silences.
Did the man my brother had never grown into

slip through the slick streets?
Footfalls turned to rain,
came out dry, and fell away.

III

I carry a desert with me.

—GEORGE GISSING

Eurydice in Florida

Marble wasn't good enough.
Gods built temples of cloud,
crowding a sky as deeply marine
as the swimming pools that jeweled backyards.

Was that thunder I heard
or the cloudiest of columns falling?
Had great dead poets put down their pens
to let rain erase what they'd written?

Love, the first night in Florida I remembered
what I'd forgotten. The second one, I began to forget.
When a god dressed in rain lay down beside me,
I let him cover me. But he couldn't rest.

He touched things you'd given me—
though I forget which.
Was it some other day where you were?
Over the street, under the sun,

fish crows cast their mourning veil.
"Oh no!" they cried to no one in particular.
The path was blocked by black umbrellas.
Vultures impatient to survey the stink of eternity

creaked dark wings open, then smacked them shut.
Not meant to walk, the birds listed. They hissed.

Down the trail, their shadows flailed and tottered,
not meant to walk. They hissed and moaned.

They eyed the living, as if to say,
Why are you here? You're not dead yet.

The Scholar's Rock

Lingbi stone, wood base, Qing dynasty

said, I love the way those old drunks wrote,
all that dew, moon, rain on bamboo, et cetera.
They wrote on paintings. They wrote on jade
to stop the knife cutting deeper.

They wrote and drank, drank and wrote.
And they always said "I,"
especially when no one was home
at the hut where they stopped
on their way to exile even more remote.

They always left a poem to say
life would likely never send them by again
but, friend, don't cut that bamboo—
no, wait till snow gives it a blanket
beautiful enough to take your breath away

from the cold, the loneliness, et cetera.
The drunken Minister on Distant Service
to Celestial Principalities, that banished immortal,
envoy on earth of the thirty-six Heavenly Rulers,
that Person in Plain Clothes

who leaned from his boat, drunk,
to scoop the dripping moon into his arms—
or so poets claim: I like him.
He drowned as a stone does, cleanly,
leaving no account.

The Monet Returns from Its Travels

I.

Away, in a room full of Monets,
I was just more of the same:

an acre of paint, a field of oats,
a summer somewhere in France.

Wild poppies tipped their papery cups
to call for light, more light,

another goblet of red, please,
though it was nowhere near noon—

last night's dregs pooled under my trees,
the blue of distance feathered the oat field,

drawing it near to push it away.

II.

I missed the way in Florida,
before the museum opens,

at the rushy rim of the pond out back,
pale yellow soup bowls of American lotus

set themselves out as if for luncheon
in the deep yellow dining room

of Monsieur l'artiste in Giverny.
Down Museum Road, mist scours Lake Alice

until it's a mirror that a great blue heron wades
into the shallows of its own reflection.

That feather of his—burnt sienna
or some shade of smoke impossible to mix?

Waiting for the next meal to swim past,
the bird holds still forever. Not so,

the blunt, smug blade of alligator
that cuts the glass into *before* and *after*.

Against Florida

Not *another* gorgeous day,
    Winter said.
You army of northern robins
    eating your way south:
Napoléon, old coot, was right.
    On your stomach
you advance, devouring berries
    left untouched
by the locals. On pyracantha
    and cabbage palm
you're drunk. You stagger into traffic
    toward a puddle
big enough for a bath. And I,

    toothless zephyr
at the Fountain of Youth Golf Course—
    the breeze in plaid pastels
who just sent a ball into the water hazard—
    eye a sly drifter,
the alligator who owns the pond.

    Hot air rising,
I embrace you. A single dance?
    Into a tornado
we could twirl, lifting roofs
    off this balmy state.
O Florida in February!
    Your perfume

of lighter fluid and tanning butter
    goes to the head.
Why am I here? At your dripping feet,
    I lay my cold heart,
soaked in your salt.

To a Glass Lizard

You know me,
packing to cross an ocean
  in search of something
overlooked in my backyard.
  Pliny was right:
Rome a Roman never sees.

You know me—
years I crossed, porch to car,
  and never saw you,
stubby snake who ruled the place.
  Speckled pretzel
able to untie itself, droopy pencil

  looped on a branch
of azalea bush like a lesson lost
  from penmanship—
when did evolution take your legs,
  glass lizard?
You'd shed two-thirds your length

  to escape,
leaving your tail thrashing
  to distract me.
Few adults are perfect, the book says,
  but the tail regrows.
Lizard, don't move. Don't break.

Let me
disappear into the underbrush
of everyday loss.

By a Pond on a Muggy Evening

First came the *quaink* of a distant cowbell,
then the *quonk* of a plucked banjo string.
A cheep, a drowsy birdlike chirp,
the basso profundo of *jug-o-rum*—

frogs of the duck pond, may I offer
a rough translation? *I'm your kind of animal,*
you croak. *I'm big and handsome.*
I own real estate.

Where's the female to isolate your call
in the jubilant, desperate din
I hear a block away? Love, stop the car.
Turn off the headlights and air-conditioning.

Roll down the window—oh,
a policeman has pulled up beside us.
He wants to know why we're creeping along.
A pair of professors, old enough to be his parents,

claiming that on their way home
from teaching a night class . . .
he can only shake his head and drive on.

Complaint of the Moon in the Provinces

after Laforgue

So a guitar moved in across the street?
I, the moon, am not what it sings
with its three chords.

Of arms and the woman, it sobs.
In the dead afternoon of the provinces,
nothing moves but a cat on the run

from the caterwaul. Onto someone else's porch
it slinks. Cat curling into a rock,
I am fire turned to stone.

But you have a voice—save it
for the night to come. Don't waste it
on the lizard turning to wood on the railing.

And you, moonflower, I see you
send out a runner in the heat.
Why the rush to clamber over an azalea bush?

Open your waxen trumpets for me.
Over shaggy palms I rise,
over swamp turned parking lot,

empty as ocean, yet floodlit.
Minor moons of street lamps must be roused,
and that moth on the screen door.

Can you read by my light? Over your shoulder,
I would bend to the moth's dusty book
and, in its lost language, see —

but, no, I'm a million miles away.
I see the scar of the Great Wall of China,
still there, on the wrinkled skin of the earth.

Today's Meditation: The Sadness
of the Subtropics

Rain won't let go this afternoon.
Palm fronds wear the water like a glove.

They don't wave: there's nothing to salute.
They shudder, they sag and spill—

and then a ghostly bark announces
to any female close enough,

not that the worst has washed over us,
but that a tree frog has had enough

to drink at last, down through his skin,
and waits for love to come to him.

Stopping by the Woods
During Bowhunting Season

I.

In the flatwoods of Florida,
one road away from the twenty-first century,
I heard birdcalls grow too big for their birds.

A cathedral of silence shattered by song—
how could such piercing praise
let fly from less than an ounce of wren?

In the shallow relief of light
carved from dark, I heard
what I couldn't see: dawn, or just after,

too late to catch what we'd come for,
a glimpse of endangered woodpecker.
That woody drumming—

II.

Was that thunder yours, my heart?
A man wearing leaves drove a truck of dust
down Gasline Road. To the hunted,

wire grass telegraphed my trampling of it.
In the understory, I found myself
royally fanned by saw palmettos—

no, I was flailed. Longleaf pines swayed
to something only they could hear.
Thirty feet up, from their eighteen-inch needles,

down came an empty sleeve of air.
Only the wood tick took me for the animal I was—
took from me deeply, under the skin.

Musica Mundana

I heard the sky before I saw it,
   the way Audubon did,
      reloading his rifle.

When I stepped from the car,
   the great bowl
      spilled the cries

of six thousand sandhill cranes
   at my unworthy feet.
      I waded the racket,

the cloudy feathers of angels
   who wintered in Florida.
      For who, given wings,

would bother with Michigan
   when you could cross
      this water meadow,

in formation, feeding as you went?
   The morning tasted of dirt
      and it was good,

worth rattling about to high heaven,
   then pecking at a neighbor
      who came too close.

O tinny seraphim! Rusty cherubim!
    The music of the spheres
        needed a crotchet,

a quaver, a mordent of WD-40.

A Classroom in Hell

It was hot and growing hotter:
every question I asked about poetry
went looking for air-conditioning.

In Florida, you needed it to think.
Life Studies and *For the Union Dead*,
open to any page, fanned unmoved air.

Those before us had gouged despair
at scaling the overlooks of learning
into the desks. Even the building

longed for the beach.
But who sat at the back in a heavy coat
a century out of date and still too big?

Someone who didn't belong there:
the ghost of my Polish grandfather,
sixteen again, staring out the window—

though there wasn't one.
When would the single day he'd spend
in school in Nebraska at last be over?

What good was geometry to the Great Plains,
where the shortest distance
between two points was always a day away?

English, his pen of pigs knew,
lacked the gristle of consonants to chew.
Come the cold, he would turn their gutturals

into coarse, garlicky sausage no words could touch.

To a Redbud

When I heard your name,
    I thought *lipstick,*
cardinal, ketchup, pigeon-blood ruby,
    something *sanguine*—

even as you flowered "purple/pink,"
    the field guide said
with an air of defeat when, finally,
    I looked you up.

You don't bother with leaves.
    Furred with petals,
you race the wild plum into bloom.
    You cloud the sky.

You're childhood's Horse Heaven Hills
    come back in dream,
dirt painted purple by dawn.
    The Greyhound bus

that no longer runs—again it trundles
    over White Pass,
the only passenger the ghost
    of my mother.

Dead two years, she loves to travel
    so lightly now.
She's puncture vine curled in her seat,
    prickly as ever—

if she still finds Seattle "excessively green,"
    she won't say.
Why am I not there to meet her?
    Even in dream,

the living keep busy, betraying the dead.
    Flowering Judas,
they call you, redbud not red.

Elegy for a Carpenter's Carpenter

in memoriam Larry Haun (1931–2011)

I. *Without*

Redwings called, weed to weed
above a lovesick alligator's low notes.

In dank remains of a lotus bed,
silence stood, white-feathered,

as tall as I was. The whooping crane
let a handful of sandhill cranes nearby

pass for family, but only to outsiders:
in a dead forest of dog fennel—

shadow palace floating—
they played courtiers to the brilliant one.

Over the fetor of Florida,
cumulus scrambled to rise.

But the tall, uncomprehending hero
said nothing. Said, *I envy*

the mosquito you don't see
reflected in the swamp-black mirror.

There is no solitude like mine.
The sky lowers itself yet does not weep.

II. *Within*

I remember his hands, wood, gouged by use,
knuckles kin to burls—hands

that did finish carpentry with a small chainsaw
as silkily as they threaded a sewing machine.

In this forest of family, no matter how hard
the rest of us grew, uncles stayed tallest.

Now in rain forest the first lies fallen.
Uncle Redwood, shrouded in fog,

I remember your emails always ended:
"Send sunlight." Someday one of us

will lay down your book, pick up a hammer,
clamber to a roof, and say to a nail,

"I won't lie. Even he would have hit you:
once to set you straight, once to drive you home."

Into a cloud of grief off the Oregon coast,
the land-sea breeze sinks a sixpenny slider,

a soft-steel glint that catches and flares.

IV

where my whole life comes haunting:
invisible van-load of furniture.

—TOMAS TRANSTRÖMER

The Way Water Does

England we walk without saying a word,
as the long-*un*married do.

Trees meet overhead in a vague Gothic arch
so green the shade needs a flying buttress.

O leafy vaults of High Perpendicular!
O waning of our middle ages!

Thirty years—no, more—since we met.
Let's stand on the fake Bridge of Sighs.

Over the sleepy Cam it bends, not quite at home,
as if the arch, raising weighty skirts

above the drag and stench of history,
should remember a side canal in Venice—

but I can't. I do. Behind the decorated cake
of Doge's Palace, crossing the real Bridge of Sighs,

I found nothing to sigh over.
Taking its time, rain has licked the faces

of Cambridge, gargoyle and angel, back to lumps.
Kissed in public by inconstant sun,

the faceless history of England blushes.
You know my skin the way water does.

Outside of Paradise

I. *The Fall of Eve*

I was eating a piece of fruit
when I heard something outside.
I called my husband.

"That hole in the sky, the 'moon,'"
he said, "won't stop moving.
The watered-down light of 'Milky Way'

trips and spills in the dark,
with nothing to sop it up.
Did you hear an angel up to no good?

No, you heard 'trees.'"
He went back to sleep. He slept for ages.
Finally, "morning" arrived,

sky scrubbed of heaven.
Trees stripped of leaf by night
tried to cover themselves. Husband slept on.

Oh, fallen apple, keep me company
as we wither and bruise. Windfall,
let me taste the worm at the heart,

I who am lower than dirt.

II. *Adam and Eve in Venice*

First waters of light
lap at the window—

was that what woke me?
Or stone-faced stillness,

air empty of birdsong?
In a strange room we lay,

you no longer a stranger
but somewhere else in dream.

Waves of sound rippled stone walls.
In a canal that stank sweetly of decay

stood a city on tiptoe. Across the campo,
footsteps picked a path bent on passing

through our room on their way to church.
Was that a heron in high heels?

Or landfall of an angel about to turn
to stone after a night on the lagoon?

Someone already late, I thought,
at this blue hour, for the rest of her life.

III. *Eve in the Fall*

Summer torn down, petal by petal—
had the father of storms spent himself at last?
An avalanche of silence fell.

My eyelids fluttered open
as they had that first morning
I saw you beside me, strangest of creatures,

the one most like me. But you were old.
When I looked closer, I saw myself
in your eyes, fallen leaf starting to turn on itself.

I heard a rustling, tree trying to shake
or river feeling its way past a wall
toward some vast body it didn't know existed.

Down the street, trucks trundled dark goods
to eternity, one red light after another.
Street lamps trudged the sidewalk

like husbands yawning their way to work.
On puddles, on unwashed cloud,
they spilled their weak, human light.

With shadow my cup overflowed.

IV. *A Cold Day in Hell*

at the butterfly house

At the gate of Eden we stood, wanting back in.
A scruffy seraph stuffed money into frayed jeans.
"Don't let them out," he said.

Did I hear a soul
as a door closed behind us?
A piece of stained glass flickered by,

then a moth more secular, wings clear as windows.
Another turned to tree bark when it landed.
A velvet eyespot stared at me until I blinked.

What could be read in that iridescent dust?
As if, in a book of devotions, years
had robbed the miniature for December

of all but sky. Gone the blond castle
that lifted expensive *azur d'outreme*
away from the bones of winter trees.

Gone the silken cloud of greyhounds,
their red rapture at the flesh they felled
for a feast called the Nativity.

The watch-spring of a tongue uncoiled.
What question did the question-mark butterfly pose,
deep in the throat of a death-scented flower?

The tattered comma had a day to live.

V. *Eve in England*

So this was the wider world:
a tiny British backyard
choked with weed, or not—

I wasn't sure.
Flowers were things you cut
and brought inside to watch die.

The blackbird, if that's what he was,
kept one eye on a cathedral of cloud,
the other on his drab mate.

The female searched,
but not for food. Up to the house
she skittered, untamed, unapproachable.

From the doormat, she pulled another tuft:
time for the second brood of the season.
Was she mending a nest or starting over?

Like a book left in the open,
blossoms swelled and spilled,
pages foxing as they came unbound.

Pages faded, losing their place:
in the kitchen, I sat where minor characters do,
scullery maid brought to life

in a single sentence of *Sleeping Beauty*,
then sent to sleep for a century.
Tears would dry on her cheek,

the cruel world of an onion
roll from a hand gone slack.
Until the day Love swept through,

looking for Beauty in a grander room:
You open your eyes. A strange man leans over you.
In the beginning. For a while.

Complaint of the Rain in English

Down the stained velvet
of swan neck, raindrops roll.
Between the great wings, they pool.

You've seen it, too, as you scurry by:
you want to cup and carry it off,
but your hands are full of holes.

I rumple the river into raw silk,
yet you want to be anywhere but here.
Where's the nearest desert?

At the heart of a droplet, I bring you
a grain of sand from the Sahara,
if you will just look up.

But you hunch in the doorway
of an English church. Though it's locked,
I've wormed my way in without a key:

frescoes peel from walls in my presence,
but—wet rat shaking on the steps,
trying to make yourself smaller—

you don't bend on drenched knee to me.
Under a leaky canopy of leaves,
collar turned up, chin against chest—

how clumsily you swim the fluent air,
though you're mostly water.
I dampen bare skin at the nape of your neck.

You don't love me, but the roses do.
From thorn to thorn, I lick my way.

Theory of the Leisure Class

Gold leaf, ground sapphire:
in the English book of hours,
the longest day turns a page in the season

of spending no sumptuary law can curb—
but today's meditation has been interrupted
by feathery clatter: wood pigeon,

stuffed into waistcoat, distracted
on the way to Ascot by some shrub at my window.
Branches too slender to bear its weight

dangle fruit almost beneath notice—barely there,
ruby umbrella tips I glimpsed in a jeweler's window
once in Venice. Who couldn't live without them?

O long-rotted silk parasol! Whisper
what those blood drops cost.
On a tag tied to the most decadent things

I'd ever seen, zeros trailed some number.
Now from the stiffest branch, craning a neck
he doesn't have, the bird still can't reach one.

Upside down, tail fanned, wings spread—
a wilder rippling shakes the other birds
down to their claws.

Then desire has lost to gravity.

Nocturne for Amphibian Voice

East of sleep, a faucet dripped.
A drop shook itself awake
in night's blackened, tinny pail—

as if, down the back alley
that cut between spring and fall,
summer had cast a daylily in bronze.

No, an ancient underwater bell,
tied to a lighthouse long dark, warned
sleep's shallow draw against the shoals of dream.

The North Sea wanted the fens back.
Through the alley's narrows something wormed—
a submarine, sonar drowsily pinging,

echolocating broken glass,
foundered masts of hollyhock.
No, neighbors would insist tomorrow,

a foreign toad has taken up residence.
They do not love you, warts and all.
Little invader, we're not native

to this island. In a voice too big
to fit inside your skin, you call, you call.

To an Oriental Poppy in an Easterly Breeze

You don't belong here, either—
you're no more English than I.

You're the Silk Route, poppy,
the Grand Bazaar, hempen sacks slit open,

spices heaped into mountains,
your passes uncharted, unstable.

Who brought you north
to battle wind from the east?

A ghost ship floats the North Sea.
On ice-crystal cloud, it sails.

Your furred green fist holds nothing
but petal, crumpled flags daring to unfurl.

How grasp this isle of sour Sundays,
where castles spin of wet leaf-smoke?

This postage stamp of British backyard
has been invaded by forget-me-nots:

at your foot, blue infantry quake.
You're more ruby than the robin

who looses a fusillade of trills.
Over crumbling back wall, a curved blade of moon.

Through an empire left unmanned,
eastern breeze has chilled the ancient seabed

from the Urals to the Pennines.
Your cup of flame? Drop by lead-crystal drop,

rain behind wind ripped your petals off.

To the One Who Wore the World's Oldest Shirt

Up dark stairs I climbed
to a museum of even greater dark.
I took the flashlight offered.

After beads strung from the backbone
of a songbird eaten in the First Dynasty,
I came to the oldest shirt in the world.

Where was he now, that teenager
who shrugged it off five thousand years ago?
He turned it inside out, pulling it over his head—

what was his hurry? Impatient one,
I saw your shirt in London yesterday.
It was found again in a heap of rags

someone hauled home
from a tomb in the Valley of the Kings.
The tomb wasn't yours, boy with no name.

But someone turned the shirt right side out.
Someone washed away your salt
and pressed what was left of the linen

into pleats again, and the ghost of pleats.
Where there were holes, in the afterlife
there's a web of silk crêpeline.

Where's the canopic jar with a jackal's head
that held your viscera?
Where's the death charm

your people would have bound
into the funeral bandage of someone so young?
So whoever entered the tomb,

her nose behind her, her face turned
toward the weak light of the upper world,

would be warned: *Run out,*
thou who comest into the dark.

The Ark in the Window

Forty days and forty nights, it rained.
In the wettest summer recorded,
rivers burst their raddled banks.
On the forty-first day, in a thrift shop window,

an ark appeared. More cardboard than boat,
it held a toy lion who'd lost an ear,
a warthog under the wing of a patchwork goose.
A matted gorilla tested the waters

some god had made by rumpling a bedsheet.
There a walrus floated, unconcerned
Noah had disappeared—unless a headless mannequin,
baby in cowhide-spotted pajamas, was patriarch.

Down an old curtain fell striped, dotty rain.
Up a scrap-lumber ramp, more warthogs jostled
a gutless hand puppet who fell on its nose.
What dry land was left? Fuzzy runnels

of pink blanket slid down a stack of books.
A tin-snipped elephant airlifted to a shelf
as waters rose regarded a North American cardinal
who looked hung over. Chased by a snakeskin swimsuit,

a fake crocodile purse barred tigerish boots.
But the hen-shaped covered dish sailed calmly on.
And it repented the Lord that he had made man on the earth.

England in the Dark Ages

Dawn refused to stagger into the light.
Out of the North Sea crawled more rain,

dragging inland, almost human.
Nailed to the overturned keel of a roof,

bare branches of a TV aerial shook
a song thrush until it launched into matins.

From some early English missal,
the bird sang to the sleepy street.

He extolled his feathered kind,
lavishing praise on one who sang in rain

lest he sing not at all. A drizzle of notes,
a mizzle, a smur—he sang buckets and pitchforks,

cats and dogs. Notes fell in stair rods,
in spit and piss. Deep in the fens,

in the riddled remains of the longboats
in which they lay, bones of ancient kings

began to stir. There were new, uncharted waters to cross,
so why stay buried, home and dry?

There were wetlands to fight into,
the suck and squelch of each miserable step

daring you deeper. On such a morning,
landlocked Ely, down the fen,

could find itself the Isle of Eels again,
cut off from everything but its past.

A dawn as dismal, as miasmal, as this,
how could anyone still sleep?

Address of the Rat
upon the Winter Solstice

Let winter gnaw the year to the bone.
Let December claw whatever moves—
a sickle moon cuts a hole in the dark
    the size of a rat.

Creatures of the alley, prick up your ears!
The longest night, carved with a lost,
a bent, a tarnished teaspoon
    from frozen dirt,

is ours. Should the Son of man think
to be born again, let him be warned:
the young and weak are here
    to be devoured.

In the churlish chill of meantime,
the tallest animal of the street—
two-legged, furless, wrapped in fake fur—
    that flightless bird

has hung bird feeders, it is true.
But do not rush to fight over the spill.
In the shed under which I burrow,
    unknown to him,

I tell you, he has left loose a tin of suet cakes.
Out of woodpile and leaf litter,

from flowerpot fallen on its side,
   crawl. Hurry!

Rat and mouse, vole or shrew,
lift the refinement of your snouts.
We are past freezing—citizens of the alley,
   we feast tonight.

A Walk Through the Ice Age

Eight hundred years of learning came unbound:
north of December, lit by a slit of sun,

whitened roofs of Cambridge stood,
single folds of paper ungathered.

Snow lay dust sheets over cars,
a street of mastodons waiting to thaw.

My shoes tried to slip from under me
and race ice crystals skating the gutter.

Watch your feet, dreamer! Don't step
on that slice of cucumber, lacy with frost.

Don't listen to that sooty smudge of bird
chipping at the flinty air—

there will be no song for a month or more,
though petals shiver on a Japanese cherry

guarding the door of the Conservative Club.
From a lost book of devotions,

here was the plate for December:
in the plumber's window, the latest fashion

in radiators huddled, a flurry of mothballs
at its feet—were they snow or hail?

The one green thing, a plastic pine tree,
bristled at being hung with copper elbows

and brassy nipples. O Christmas Eve!
The bookbinder didn't want to rebind a thing,

or creak a hand-cranked guillotine to life.
But he would trim a ream down to a size

no longer manufactured, were that all I wanted.
A yowl from the Iron Age emerged, unrusted.

Unfed for eons, the great maw yawned,
then drank a single drop of oil

under the glacial gaze of pinups
too scantily clad for that cold cavern,

their airbrushed acres of skin, scraped and tanned,
gone yellow and parchment-brittle.

Raw Ode

I.

Winter, with each woolly breath,
I have been unfaithful. Wearing next to nothing,

I have lain in Florida sun in February.
I was in another country,

and besides, it's you I love.
Teach me to read the darkest page,

the one you turn just before dawn.

II.

Sleepers! the robin calls. *Bring out your knives!*
Bird, I would sing the things that burn:

the quince petal's first flush.
It will not last the night. The last rosebud—

wind, don't knock down its small door.
Don't waste your icy breath

on that pile of black-damp leaves.
A buried ember feathers its grave with ash.

On Being Fiftysomething

From thirty to forty, you're distracted
by the five lusts, which I don't need to go into.
From seventy to eighty, you're prone
to a hundred diseases or more.

Who can remember their names,
or the ones of friends who've gone
and died on you? But from fifty to sixty,
you're free of all that.

Grief doesn't know where you live yet,
only gravity, the body starting to sag
under the weight of memories that,
like extra pounds around the middle,

you can't seem to lose. At the theater, you doze,
your eyelids curtains that refuse to stay raised.
Suddenly, you're director of a play
about to start. Time: none like the present.

Place: a room you think you recognize.
On the desk, a typewriter squats like a toad,
waiting for a word.
The wall's the wrong color,

but its painted muslin quivers:
from backstage someone tries the door,

which refuses to give. How young you were,
the overbright shabbiness all yours,

that desert full of dream.

Romeo, the Morning After

Two by two, the houses shared a wall,
as if forced to touch for the sake

of a long-lost photograph.
"Semidetached," the British called them,

the houses feeling neither here nor there
about such a marriage, or such a street,

keeping their eyes shut, curtains drawn—
except for an upper window agape.

After a night in a bed not his,
a young man climbed into morning, one floor up.

Black as asphalt, a bird claimed an aerial.
But soft, what light!

Shakespearean in their twists and trills,
his tarred and melting notes laid out

a tale of two birds we walked beneath,
turning the corner, Love, from Saturday

to middle age. No longer were we the young
who played at love and death, then rose

and shrugged back into yesterday's clothes.

To a Book in a Window

Deep in the archives of damp they call July,
the English palimpsest suffered another layer of green
to be laid on another scraping-down.

Somer is comen and winter gon.
The isle warmed just enough
for the rented room across the street

to prop a window open with a paperback—
whose tale, long-winded,
tacked into waters not foreshadowed:

"Rain," the radio said, "will turn to showers."
Book, teach me the difference.
Your pages soak and swell,

voluminous frill whose fore edge foxes.
A coat outgrown, your cover shrinks
from words it wrapped itself around.

Story of my life, where do you wander?
Down the street, a muezzin calls
from the old Methodist chapel.

And there I am, about to turn the corner
into my sixties, longing to be a skin,
wet skin, scraped clean again.

ACKNOWLEDGMENTS

The American Scholar: "Windy Ode"

Antioch Review: "England in the Dark Ages," "Without"

The Atlantic Monthly: "Expression of Emotion in Man and In-sects," "On Being Fiftysomething," "Today's Meditation: The Sadness of the Subtropics"

Cambridge Literary Review: "The Scholar's Rock"

The Hopkins Review: "Address of the Rat upon the Winter Sol-stice," "Eve in England," "To a Glass Lizard"

The Hudson Review: "A Cold Day in Hell," "Elegy for an English Teacher"

Idaho Review: "May Altar Constructed from Memory," "My First Museum"

Kenyon Review: "Complaint of the Rain in English"

Literary Imagination: "The Later Martyrs," "Double Self-Portrait, Pinned Together"

The New Criterion: "Eve in the Fall," "The Family Silence," "Theory of the Leisure Class"

New England Review: "Eurydice in Florida," *"Flora Americana,"* "House Spider's Odyssey," "In the Museum of Recent Time," *"Musica Mundana,"* "To an Oriental Poppy in an Easterly Breeze," "To a Redbud," "Within"

The Paris Review: "Raw Ode"

Poetry: "Complaint of the Moon in the Provinces"

Poetry Northwest: "A Walk Through the Ice Age"

Raritan: "A Classroom in Hell," "On First Looking into Darwin's Microscope," "Stopping by the Woods During Bowhunting Season," "To a Mockingbird by the Rappahannock," "The War After the War"

Salmagundi: "Adam and Eve in Venice," "Against Florida," "To Myself, Then"

Samuel P. Harn Museum of Art at Twenty Years (University Press of Florida, 2010): "The Monet Returns from Its Travels," "The Scholar's Rock"

The Sewanee Review: "Surplus Poem," "Thrush's Song," "The Way Water Does"

The Southern Review: "Prelude and Fugue for Desert Winds"

Southwest Review: "The Ark in the Window"

TriQuarterly: "By a Pond on a Muggy Evening," "The Fall of Eve," "Keats to a Young Poet of the Seventies," "The Last Dodo of Iowa," "My Brief Reign"

Virginia Quarterly Review: "Elegy on the Far Bank" (sections II–V)

The Warwick Review: "In Darwin's Room," "Nocturne for Amphibian Voice"

The Yale Review: "Elegy on the Far Bank" (section I), "On First Looking into Chapman's *Flora*," "Romeo, the Morning After," "To a Book in a Window"

Debora Greger is the author of ten books of poetry. She lives in Gainesville, Florida, where she is poet in residence at the Harn Museum of Art, and in Cambridge, England.

JOHN ASHBERY
Selected Poems
Self-Portrait in a Convex Mirror

PAUL BEATTY
Joker, Joker, Deuce

JOSHUA BENNETT
The Sobbing School

TED BERRIGAN
The Sonnets

LAUREN BERRY
The Lifting Dress

PHILIP BOOTH
Lifelines: Selected Poems 1950–1999

JULIANNE BUCHSBAUM
The Apothecary's Heir

JIM CARROLL
Fear of Dreaming: The Selected Poems
Living at the Movies
Void of Course

ALISON HAWTHORNE DEMING
Genius Loci
Rope
Stairway to Heaven

CARL DENNIS
Another Reason
Callings
New and Selected Poems 1974–2004
Practical Gods
Ranking the Wishes
Unknown Friends

DIANE DI PRIMA
Loba

STUART DISCHELL
Dig Safe

STEPHEN DOBYNS
Velocities: New and Selected Poems:
1966–1992

EDWARD DORN
Way More West

ROGER FANNING
The Middle Ages

ADAM FOULDS
The Broken Word

CARRIE FOUNTAIN
Burn Lake
Instant Winner

AMY GERSTLER
Crown of Weeds
Dearest Creature
Ghost Girl
Medicine
Nerve Storm
Scattered at Sea

EUGENE GLORIA
Drivers at the Short-Time Motel
Hoodlum Birds
My Favorite Warlord

DEBORA GREGER
By Herself
Desert Fathers, Uranium Daughters

God
In Darwin's Room
Men, Women, and Ghosts
Western Art

TERRANCE HAYES
Hip Logic
How to Be Drawn
Lighthead
Wind in a Box

NATHAN HOKS
The Narrow Circle

ROBERT HUNTER
Sentinel and Other Poems

MARY KARR
Viper Rum

JACK KEROUAC
Book of Blues
Book of Haikus
Book of Sketches

JOANNA KLINK
Circadian
Excerpts from a Secret Prophecy
Raptus

JOANNE KYGER
As Ever: Selected Poems

ANN LAUTERBACH
Hum
If in Time: Selected Poems,
1975–2000
On a Stair
Or to Begin Again
Under the Sign

CORINNE LEE
Plenty

PHILLIS LEVIN
May Day
Mercury
Mr. Memory & Other Poems

PATRICIA LOCKWOOD
Motherland Fatherland
Homelandsexuals

WILLIAM LOGAN
Macbeth in Venice
Madame X
Strange Flesh
The Whispering Gallery

ADRIAN MATEJKA
The Big Smoke
Map to the Stars
Mixology

MICHAEL MCCLURE
Huge Dreams: San Francisco and
Beat Poems

ROSE MCLARNEY
Its Day Being Gone

DAVID MELTZER
David's Copy: The Selected Poems
of David Meltzer

ROBERT MORGAN
Dark Energy
Terroir

CAROL MUSKE-DUKES
An Octave above Thunder
Red Trousseau
Twin Cities

ALICE NOTLEY
Certain Magical Acts
Culture of One
The Descent of Alette
Disobedience
In the Pines
Mysteries of Small Houses

WILLIE PERDOMO
The Essential Hits of Shorty Bon Bon

LIA PURPURA
It Shouldn't Have Been Beautiful

LAWRENCE RAAB
The History of Forgetting
Visible Signs: New and Selected
Poems

BARBARA RAS
The Last Skin
One Hidden Stuff

MICHAEL ROBBINS
Alien vs. Predator
The Second Sex

PATTIANN ROGERS
Generations
Holy Heathen Rhapsody
Quickening Fields
Wayfare

ROBYN SCHIFF
A Woman of Property

WILLIAM STOBB
Absentia
Nervous Systems

TRYFON TOLIDES
An Almost Pure Empty Walking

SARAH VAP
Viability

ANNE WALDMAN
Gossamurmur
Kill or Cure
Manatee/Humanity
Structure of the World Compared
to a Bubble

JAMES WELCH
Riding the Earthboy 40

PHILIP WHALEN
Overtime: Selected Poems

ROBERT WRIGLEY
Anatomy of Melancholy and Other
Poems
Beautiful Country
Box
Earthly Meditations: New and
Selected Poems
Lives of the Animals
Reign of Snakes

MARK YAKICH
The Importance of Peeling Potatoes
in Ukraine
Unrelated Individuals Forming a
Group Waiting to Cross